THE WAY OF CAIN

BREAKING THE CYCLE OF SELF-DECEPTION

The Way of Cain
ISBN 978-1-936314-55-3

Copyright © 2011
by Dr. Billy J. Rash

Billy Rash Ministries
7850 White Lane, No. 117
Bakersfield, California 93309

Published by Word and Spirit Books
P.O. Box 701403
Tulsa, Oklahoma 74170

THE WAY OF CAIN

BREAKING THE CYCLE OF SELF-DECEPTION

BY DR. BILLY J. RASH

DEDICATION

This book is dedicated to my wife and best friend, Shelby Rash, and to my spiritual parents, Kenneth and Gloria Copeland. Without their love, patience, and instruction in the Word, I would not be in ministry today.

A special thank you goes to my Marine Corps prophet and friend, Dr. Mark Barclay, *Semper Fi*, and another prophet of God and friend, Dr. Jerry Savelle.

A special thank you also goes to Michelle Byerly for her work transcribing, editing, and her assistance in putting this book into a format that can be read and understood.

CONTENTS

Foreword

My spiritual father, Oral Roberts, once made a simple, yet so very powerful, statement that changed the way I think. Brother Roberts said, "God has never created something or someone to be something He has already forbidden! If He were to do that, He would be part of a terrible, heart-breaking situation."

If God declares something forbidden—such as stealing, calling it sin—and then He creates someone to be a thief, what chance of any kind of salvation does that person have? Especially since "the wages of sin is death." A person may think, feel, dress, act, and in many other ways be a thief, but it is not God who made him that way. Someone might say, "But I have been that way all of my life." That is still not the issue. Proverbs 14:12 boldly states, *There is a way that seems right to a man, but its end is the way of death.*" Billy Rash's book, *The Way of Cain*, is a shining floodlight beacon on that previously dark, deadly road. GET OFF OF IT AND STAY OFF!

READ THIS BOOK! Check out every Scripture verse, then read it again and put every word into action. **This is one of those "Wow, I never knew that!" books.** It opens one's eyes to the WAY that is right for any man, woman, or child to lead an abundant life. Billy quotes Jesus as saying, "I have come that you might enjoy LIFE and have it in abundance to the full, till it overflows." Oh, thank God for no more dark roads leading to heartbreak and death. No more curse!

Thank you, Billy Rash, for such a powerful tool for our faith and deliverance. **This WAY works!** Ask Gloria and me how we know. We have lived it for forty-five years.

JESUS IS LORD,

Kenneth Copeland
Kenneth Copeland Ministries
Fort Worth, Texas

Words from a Fellow Minister

I absolutely love this book! In fact, after reading the manuscript, I wish I had written it myself. What a wonderful job you have done, Billy. I pray every Christian everywhere will read it and meditate in the truths found on every page.

The spirit of Cain has always been of interest to me and has been one of the stories I have studied over and over again. Not only have I read about it in the Bible, but I have also seen it many times throughout my preaching career. That's right. I have seen this spirit on many modern people, and yes, even on God's people.

Obviously Pastor Billy has witnessed these same things. We have seen people who, like Cain, deal with the altar and the offering without honor, respect, or biblical order. I have found there is an absolute and definite reason why the Lord wants everything done the way He wants it done. Anyone who takes matters into their own hands and practices biblical truths in their own way, rather than God's way, always makes a mess of everything.

This is exactly what happens to people when they decide, like Cain, to serve God any way they want, rather than the way God says. As Pastor Billy brings out in this book, Cain knew to do right. He knew how to please God and receive God's blessing. He had been to the altars of God time and again, presenting his offering, and God blessed him. One time he behaved differently and presented his offering with an independent spirit and almost an attitude of belligerence. Of course, when one is mad at God, they never take it out on God. They always take it out on their brother.

This book, *The Way of Cain,* is the kind of book that needs to be read more than once. I highly recommend that you look up every verse and meditate a few moments while examining your own heart in these very issues. I agree with you, in Jesus' name, that as you read this book, the Holy Spirit will reveal to you and help you correct any area of your life that may be following after the way of Cain. Such correction will allow you to escape the horrible and painful repercussions of allowing this evil spirit and ungrateful attitude to strip your life of the protections and blessings of God.

Thank you, my dear Brother Billy, for allowing the Holy Spirit to use you to write this book. I respect you for it. May it change a multitude of lives and make an open shame of our adversary, the Devil.

Dr. Mark T. Barclay
Preacher of Righteousness
Midland, Michigan

A Special Note

Billy's new book is so timely for these tumultuous times. He shares often ignored—but powerful—truths about our walk with Christ and the deception and subtlety of the Devil.

He clearly outlines God's instructions for keeping ourselves in His perfect will—free of error and free from the Devil's snares. He reveals the seductions we face, how to recognize the enemy's strategies, and how to lay hold of God's principles that enable us to walk victoriously. I know that as you apply these principles, you will be blessed, strengthened, encouraged, and ready for the challenges that come your way; you will be positioned for victorious living in these last days!

Dr. Jerry Savelle
Jerry Savelle Ministries International
Crowley, Texas

THE WAY OF CAIN

Introduction

As the pastor of a church, I often have ministers come to me seeking counsel. As of late, many pastors are becoming increasingly concerned for church members who, although once faithful and committed, seem to be no longer connected with the church. They have stopped giving, attending services, and supporting the ministries they once did. It appears this portion of their congregation has slipped into a spiritual apathy that has blinded their minds to the very truths they once walked.

Such apathy, which is my purpose for writing this book, is a dangerous spiritual condition affecting the Body of Christ. It is a self-deceiving spiritual attitude called the **way of Cain.** The cause and manifestations of the **way of Cain** may surprise you.

Throughout this study, you will be called upon to make a **choice**. It is my prayer that you choose God's way, which is the **way of life.**

CHAPTER 1

Choose Life

In the book of Deuteronomy, God advises the children of Israel to "choose life." The Lord says,

> *"I call heaven and earth as witnesses* ["to record" KJV] *today against you, that I have set before you life and death, blessing and cursing; therefore* **choose life,** *that both you and your descendants may live."*
>
> Deuteronomy 30:19

Who in their right mind would choose death or a curse?

Why do you suppose God would have to alert His people to make such a choice? Is there a chance someone might choose something other than life? Who in their right mind would choose death or a curse?

Yet throughout the Old Testament, we find the children of Israel **not** choosing life, but choosing cursing and death. Why would they do that even after God told them which to choose?

Through the Scripture, God presents us with the same choice today. Clearly there are those who will, and do, choose wrongly or God would not advise us to do otherwise.

What about you? If Jesus himself appeared in bodily form and said to you, "I set before you life (blessing) and death (cursing). Which do you want? And, by the way, if you are not sure which is best, I will tell you: It is life! The Father and I want you to choose life so that you and your descendants can be blessed." Which would you choose?

If a choice must be made, then it is safe to assume that life and blessings will not automatically jump on us, even as Christians, simply because it is available. We have to make a **choice**. We must **choose** life and blessing.

As the end-time draws nearer to its conclusion, we as believers are *called to record,* to make a choice. Because of the high stakes of this choice, every evil force is trying to blind and hinder you from making the right choice. Jesus gave us the correct answer: **CHOOSE LIFE.**

Now listen carefully, there are some people in your life who may make the *wrong* choice. *You* might make the wrong choice on occasion. Nevertheless, we still have to choose.

As a pastor, it is my responsibility to equip you with the spiritual tools necessary to make the **right choice** (life and blessing). However, it is also important to examine *why* people make wrong choices.

Why Do People Make Wrong Choices?

I dare say everyone at one time or another has gone the wrong direction. The result of which was not a blessing, but a curse. There are also those who seem to make wrong choices consistently. We see it all around us. The consequences appear in almost every aspect of our lives in some form. This is not necessarily because of *your* wrong choice, but possibly the wrong choices of those around you.

My question is this: Why do people make wrong choices? Those who do not know God's Word may make wrong choices in ignorance, but what about those of us who know the Word? Why would we make the wrong choice after being warned?

With the help of the Holy Spirit, we will examine this question. With the anointing of the Holy Spirit, and with a holy boldness, I will sound the alarm of what is trying to blind you from the blessings God has for you.

The Two Men of Jeremiah

The book of Jeremiah chapter 17 gives us a sterling example of why people make the wrong choice (choosing death and cursing) even though they know the right choice (choosing life and blessing).

Verses 5-8 identify two different men. Both of these men follow the Lord, yet one chooses life and one chooses death. Beginning in verse 5, we will examine the characteristics of the first man.

*"Thus says the LORD: 'Cursed is the man who trusts in man and makes flesh his strength, whose heart **departs** from the LORD.'"*

Notice the word "departs." The man's heart was once *with* the Lord or it could not *depart*. Continuing with verse 6:

"For he shall be like a shrub ["heath" KJV] in the desert . . ."

A heath is a little, dinky dead-looking shrub that can live, basically, without anything.

"For he shall be like a shrub in the desert, and shall not see when good comes . . ."

Notice "good comes" to the man, but he does "not see" the good things. The goodness of God flows right by him, and he misses it.

The same is true of you and me. The goodness of God will come directly toward us. If you do not see the good, do not think for a minute that God is withholding anything. God's goodness, blessings, and life come right by this man, but the Scripture says his condition causes him not to recognize it.

The goodness of God will come directly toward us.

*". . . and shall **not see when good comes**, but shall inhabit the parched places in the wilderness, in a salt land which is not inhabited."*

Continuing with verse 7:

"Blessed is the man who trusts in the LORD, and whose hope is the LORD."

Now we see the condition of the second man who trusts in the Lord. He is blessed. His trust is not in man or the flesh; his trust is in the Lord. He makes a different choice.

> *"Blessed is the man **who trusts in the LORD**, and whose hope is the LORD. For he shall be like a tree planted by the waters, which spreads out its roots by the river, and will not fear when heat comes; but its leaf will be green, and will not be anxious in the year of drought, nor will cease from yielding fruit."*

This verse does not say that trouble will not come. It says that *when* trouble comes he will not be bothered. He will still yield fruit because he sees the goodness, blessings, and life. The first man departs from the Lord and does not see the goodness, blessings, and life.

Two Men—Two Different Choices

This passage of Scripture in Jeremiah describes two men who make two different choices. Supposedly, both have a heart for God, and both are available for the blessings of God; however, both have a choice.

By choosing to trust in man and not God, the first man chooses death and cursing. He does not even recognize good when it comes to him. As a result, he lives in a dry, parched place.

By choosing to trust God, the second man chooses life and blessings. His hope is in the Lord. He is not anxious or in fear. No matter what comes at him, he is still fruitful.

What Blinds the First Man?

As we examine the unfortunate condition of the first man, we must ask ourselves this question: What would make a person not see the blessing and goodness of God when it comes right by them? On the other hand, what would make a person see the goodness and blessings of God, yet do nothing? Instead of choosing blessings they choose fear, anxiety, trusting man, and drought!

We all have known people who come to church believing God for a word, hear the word, and still not receive or act on the word that comes. The answer is given, but the person does not receive it. What makes a person respond this way?

Although we will develop this answer further in the book, I will go ahead and tell you why: It is a manifestation of the *way of Cain.*

What would make a person not see the blessing and goodness of God when it comes right by them?

THAT WHICH BLINDS YOU TO NOT SEE GOOD WHEN IT COMES IS THE WAY OF CAIN

Blessings and curses, life and death, flow around you every day of your life. Which will you choose? Will you see the good when it comes? It is my prayer you will not only receive this word of choosing life, but put it into operation!

CHAPTER 2

The Way of Cain

The foundational Scriptures for this study are found in the book of Jude:

*"Woe to them! For they have gone in the **way of Cain**, have run greedily in the error of Balaam for profit, and perished in the rebellion of Korah."*

Jude 11

The word "way" in the original Greek is *hodos*, which means a journey, path, or natural road and a course of conduct or way of thinking. The "way of Cain" is a course of spiritual conduct based on wrong thinking.

Continuing with Jude 12:

*"These are **spots in your love feasts**, while they feast with you without fear, serving only*

themselves. They are clouds without water, carried about by the winds; late autumn trees without fruit, twice dead, pulled up by the roots."

The way of Cain is a spiritual attitude that allows Cain to become self-deceived.

We will discover in Chapter 5 that "spots in your love feast" are deceptions. So, when you put these two verses together, we learn that the source of Cain's thought process is *deception.*

The way of Cain is a spiritual attitude that allows Cain to become self-deceived.

How does this happen?

The Principle of Seedtime and Harvest

Everything in the kingdom of God operates on the principle of seedtime and harvest. Jesus says that everything starts with a seed:

"The kingdom of God is as if a man should scatter seed on the ground, and should sleep by night and rise by day, and the seed should sprout and grow, he himself does not know how.

"For the earth yields crops by itself: first the blade, then the head, after that the full grain in the head. But when the grain ripens, immediately he puts in the sickle, because the harvest has come."

Mark 4:26-29

In this passage, Jesus explains how a seed begins the growth process. It takes time. The same is true spiritually. Cain did not wake up one morning self-deceived and decided to think and act wrongly. It was a process. Self-deception gained momentum through a spiritual progression. This same progression is easily seen in John 10:10.

Self-deception gained momentum through a spiritual progression.

If I ask someone to quote John 10:10 off the top of their head, most people will quote, "The thief comes to **kill, steal, and destroy**," but it is not written that way. Take special notice of the order of destruction the thief attempts to accomplish:

*"The thief does not come except to **steal**, and to **kill**, and to **destroy**. I have come that they may have life, and that they may have it more abundantly."*

The spiritual progression is (1) to **steal**, (2) then **kill**, (3) and then **destroy**.

All theologians agree that Jesus says, *"I have come that they may have life, and that they may have it more abundantly."* This is speaking about the abundant spiritual life you received from Jesus Christ. It is life overflowing. That is a positive *spiritual* progression upon which everyone can agree. However, when the same theologians interpret the first part of the verse, it seems they want to turn a spiritual interpretation into a *naturalized* interpretation.

The progression in John 10:10 is the progression of spiritual things and the way they work in your life. The thief comes to "steal . . . kill . . . destroy" in that order. That is his process of affecting you. That is how he works. He (1) steals the Word, thereby (2) killing your faith, hope, confidence, and right standing with God, thus (3) destroying the blessing that is on you.

The word "kill" in this Scripture does not mean "to murder." It actually comes from the Greek word *thuo*, which means to offer or sacrifice firstfruits to a god. Interestingly, the word *thuo* is also used to describe the sacrifice of our Lord Jesus Christ, denoting a parallel with a firstfruits offering:

> *"For indeed Christ, our Passover, was sacrificed* [firstfruits offering] *for us."*
>
> 1 Corinthians 5:7

By using the word *thuo* in this instance, we gain more understanding as to the importance and reverence of a firstfruits offering. If God the Father would give His best, we must give ours. We gather from this Scripture that Cain's spiritual attitude was not irreverent necessarily, but lackadaisical in his approach.

Spiritual Firstfruits

Let us take a closer look at the word "firstfruits." It comes from the Greek word *aparche*. When the term is used to describe *spiritual* firstfruits, we see that the Holy Spirit himself, being in the presence of a believer, is a firstfruits result of what Jesus did on the Cross (Romans 8:23). In other words, the Holy Spirit is a firstfruits benefit to the Body of Christ because Jesus died on the Cross.

How important firstfruits seem to be!

The Devil Wants to
Steal Your Firstfruits

John 10:10 states that Satan comes to STEAL, KILL (the sacrifice of firstfruits), therein DESTROYING the blessing in your life. To break it down even further: Satan comes to steal your sacrifice of firstfruits

Satan comes to steal your sacrifice of firstfruits to God in order to destroy your right standing with Him.

to God in order to destroy your right standing with Him.

Right here is the spiritual progression and order of the way Satan comes and operates against you. He comes to you and tries to get an open door in order to ruin, stop, and destroy the blessings in your life. He wants to destroy your walk in faith, hope, and the proper dictates of the Word. It is a progressive order. The *Amplified Bible* reads this way:

The thief comes only in order to steal and kill and destroy. I came that they may have and enjoy life, and have it in abundance (to the full, till it overflows).

Today's English Version of the Holy Bible reads:

The thief comes only in order to steal, kill, and destroy. I have come in order that you might have life—life in all its fullness.

Notice the phrase "in order" featured in both versions. We assume this phrase means WHY Satan comes, but it also means "the order" in which Satan comes. It is saying, Satan will come in this consecutive order:

STEAL – KILL – DESTROY

That is the spiritual order and progression. Make a mental note of that order. When the thief comes: (1) he steals the Word, thereby (2) killing your faith, hope, confidence, and right standing with God, so (3) he can destroy the blessing that is *on you* as promised through the Word.

In order to see how this spiritual progression developed into the way of Cain, we must first examine the Sin of Adam and the Sin of Cain. From there, we must examine ourselves to see if this spiritual progression has taken place in our own lives.

CHAPTER 3

The Sin of Adam

The story of Adam and Eve eating the forbidden fruit is a lesson taught very early in Sunday School. We all know the story.

Adam and Eve are placed in the Garden of Eden and instructed by God to eat fruit from any tree save one: The Tree of the Knowledge of Good and Evil. Deceived by the serpent, Eve eats from the forbidden tree. Adam, although not deceived, also eats from it. This is known as the *original sin*.

Our focus for this study is to determine (1) Adam's purpose for being placed in the garden, and (2) identify the sin that he committed. Hint: the Sin of Adam may *not* be what you think.

Let us read the account in Genesis chapter 2, beginning with verse 8:

"The LORD God planted a garden eastward in Eden, and there He put the man whom He had formed [Adam and Eve]. *And out of the ground the LORD God made every tree grow that is pleasant to the sight and good for food. The tree of life was also in the midst of the garden, and the tree of the knowledge of good and evil.*

"Now a river went out of Eden to water the garden, and from there it parted and became four riverheads. The name of the first is Pishon; it is the one which skirts the whole land of Havilah, where there is gold. And the gold of that land is good. Bdellium and the onyx stone are there. The name of the second river is Gihon; it is the one which goes around the whole land of Cush. The name of the third river is Hiddekel; it is the one which goes toward the east of Assyria. The fourth river is the Euphrates.

"Then the LORD God took the man and put him in the garden of Eden to **tend and keep it.***"*

Genesis 2:8-15

God creates the Garden of Eden and places Adam and Eve in the midst of it. Adam is placed in the garden with a purpose, which is revealed in verse 15:

He is to "tend and keep it." The word "keep" used in this instance means "guard" in Hebrew.

The *King James Version* says he is to "dress it and keep it." "Dress" and "keep" are the same Hebrew words for "cultivate" and "harvest."

Other translations say he is to *"cultivate it and to guard it"* (TEV) and *"care for it and work it"* (NCV™). The *New Jerusalem Bible,* which is considered to be one of the most accurate translations, says this:

> *"Yahweh God took the man and settled him in the garden of Eden to cultivate and take care of it."*

Adam has a job. He is to cultivate, harvest, and guard the Garden of Eden. There is much fruit being produced. It is a beautiful, perfectly-watered garden made by God himself:

Adam has a job. He is to cultivate, harvest, and guard the Garden of Eden.

> *"A mist went up from the earth and watered the whole face of the ground."*
>
> Genesis 2:6

Imagine all of the fruit being produced! What is to become of it all? Is it to ripen and fall to the ground and rot? Certainly, not. It is to be cultivated, kept, watched, guarded, and then *harvested*. This is how Adam and Eve are to eat and live; they are to eat of the harvested fruit.

The Tree of the Knowledge of Good and Evil

Adam is also to tend, guard, and harvest the Tree of the Knowledge of Good and Evil. "What?" you may ask. "I thought Adam and Eve were supposed to leave that tree alone?"

Scripture does not say that Adam is put in the garden to cultivate, guard, and harvest all the trees EXCEPT the Tree of the Knowledge of Good and Evil. No, he is placed there to cultivate and harvest ALL OF THE GARDEN.

Obviously, God could see to any necessary gardening Himself; however, it is God's choice for a man to cultivate the ground of the earth.

"This is the history of the heavens and the earth when they were created, in the day that the LORD God made the earth and the heavens, before any plant of the field was in the earth and before any herb of the field had grown. For the

*LORD God had not caused it to rain on the earth, and **there was no man to till the ground.***"

Genesis 2:4-5

Before Adam, there was no earthly vessel to till the ground. Why do you suppose God would want the ground cultivated? The answer is found in Genesis chapter 8:

*"While the earth remains, **seedtime and harvest**, cold and heat, winter and summer, and day and night **shall not cease.**"*

Genesis 8:22

God tells Adam to cultivate and harvest the garden because the entire earth is based on the principle of seedtime and harvest. Not until Adam, was there a man to watch over this process. It is Adam's job, call, and purpose to cultivate, harvest, and guard the fruit of the garden; it is the reason for him being placed there (Genesis 2:5, 15).

Seedtime and Harvest

As we studied in Chapter 2, everything in the kingdom of God is based on the principle of seedtime and harvest. That is why Jesus says that if you do not understand the parable of the sower, you will not understand any of the other parables (Mark 4:13-14). Adam is to plant seed and till the ground just as we are to sow the seed of God's Word. Both will produce a harvest.

Further, Adam is to guard and cultivate the garden for the purpose of harvest time. It is God's intention for the earth to be blessed of the harvest. At harvest time in the Garden of Eden, Adam is supposed to pick the fruit from ALL the trees INCLUDING the fruit from the Tree of the Knowledge of Good and Evil. Never is he told **not** to harvest it. For that matter, never is he told not to touch it. The following is what God says concerning the trees of the Garden of Eden:

"And out of the ground the LORD God made every tree grow that is pleasant to the sight and good for food. **The tree of life was also in the midst of the garden, and the tree of the knowledge of good and evil.**

"Then the Lord God took the man and put him in the garden of Eden [the entire garden] *to tend* [cultivate] *and keep it* [harvest and guard]. *And the LORD God commanded the man, saying, 'Of every tree of the garden you may freely eat; but of the tree of the knowledge of good and evil you shall*

*not eat, for in the day that you eat of it you
shall surely die.'"*

Genesis 2:9, 15-17

Adam is told to tend, cultivate, keep, harvest, and
guard the Garden of Eden. When harvest time comes
(when you can actually eat the fruit), he is supposed to
pick the fruit from ALL the trees in the garden. This
includes the fruit of the Tree of the Knowledge of Good
and Evil. Why do you think we assume that Adam is
to leave that tree alone? Most likely because of Eve's
dialogue with the serpent. Eve says to the serpent,

*"But of the fruit of the tree which is in the
midst of the garden, God has said, 'You shall
not eat it, **nor shall you touch it,** lest you die.'"*

Genesis 3:3

Eve is deceived. God never tells her or Adam not
to touch the tree. He tells them not to eat of it. How
can you cultivate and harvest a tree if you do not
touch it? That is not what God said.

The Scripture says Adam and Eve are supposed to
harvest ALL of the trees, but of the Tree of the
Knowledge of Good and Evil, God says, in the Hebrew,
"That is My tree, do not eat of it." However, they are
assigned to cultivate it, pick the fruit, and then
present it back unto God as a **firstfruits offering**.

43

Importance of Firstfruits

Just as God provides seed to the sower (2 Corinthians 9:10), God provides a firstfruits offering for Adam and Eve to sacrifice. Why? So they can begin operating in the principle of seedtime and harvest on the earth. They are learning how to operate in natural seedtime (tilling the ground) and harvest (eating the fruit) as well as spiritual seedtime (making firstfruits offerings to God) and harvest (blessings that follow). God wants them to be blessed. This is how the system of seedtime and harvest works.

The Tree of the Knowledge of Good and Evil is a firstfruits offering to God.

The Tree of the Knowledge of Good and Evil is a firstfruits offering to God. God does not need the fruit. God designed the Tree of the Knowledge of Good and Evil as His tree for the purpose of firstfruits offerings.

As we will learn a little later in this Chapter, the book of Malachi chapter 3 addresses the Sin of Adam. God says in Malachi 3:7, *"Return unto Me, and I will return to you"* (KJV). God is saying, "Bring that fruit as a firstfruits offering, return it to Me, and as you return it to Me, I will bless it and return it to you." God makes it so easy for them; Adam is simply to return to God what was His to begin with, in the form of an offering.

What happens? Adam and Eve eat the fruit. They eat the firstfruits offering that is to be offered up to God. They eat their seed. Adam takes what is designated to be God's. What does it mean when you take something that does not belong to you? It is called STEALING.

Adam steals the firstfruits, which are God's. And when he steals the firstfruits, it starts a spiritual progression unto death:

Adam steals the firstfruits, which are God's.

"But of the tree of the knowledge of good and evil you shall not eat, for in the day that you eat of it you shall surely die."

Genesis 2:17

Adam's Original Sin Was Stealing from God

Adam should have harvested the fruit from God's tree and made a firstfruits offering to God. When you return to God what is God's, He returns to you. God would have said "Come and dine with

45

Me at the Master's table." God would have returned it back to Adam.

Remember the progression discussed in Chapter 2: steal—kill—destroy. When you start stealing, you will find yourself partaking of that which is not yours. You will find that your relationship with God is not where it should be, and then the next thing you know, it is destroying the blessings in your life. Why? Because "Return unto Me, and I will return unto you" is a spiritual fact and principle of God.

Malachi and the Sin of Adam

The book of Malachi further explains the Sin of Adam. Chapter 3 gives valuable insight into some fundamental principles of God and what it is that Adam does so wrongly.

In Malachi 3:6, God says,

*"I am the LORD, **I do not change;** there-fore you are not consumed, O sons of Jacob."*

This is how the Sin of Adam applies to us today. God says, "I do not change." Notice God tells us in the last book of the Old Testament—Malachi—that He does not change. Remember, after the close of the Old Testament, God does not speak for four hundred years.

At this point and time why does God say, *"I am the LORD, I change not"* (KJV)? Because God is the same at the beginning of the Old Testament, and He is the same at the end of the Old Testament. The Old Testament starts with the Sin of Adam, and it is ends with the same sin having to be addressed.

God is saying, "I am the same today as I was in the day of Adam. My ideas and principles are all the same. I was the same before Adam, with Adam, and now. I was the same with your fathers, and I will be the same tomorrow. I AM THE LORD. I DO NOT, WILL NOT, HAVE NOT, AND NEVER WILL CHANGE."

If God has always been the same, then these principles were in place with Adam in the Garden of Eden:

> *"Even from the days of your fathers ye are gone away from mine ordinances, and have not kept them. Return unto me, and I will return unto you, saith the LORD of hosts. But ye said, Wherein shall we return?"*
>
> Malachi 3:7, KJV

When God says to Adam, "This is My tree, return it to me and I will return to you," He means it. Some believe this passage means turning back to God in terms of salvation; however, this verse is not speaking of salvation. Here, God is not saying, "Turn back to Me and get saved," even though that is a true principle carried out in other places of Scripture.

If God is referring to salvation in this passage, or something along that line, He would not follow with the "robbing" aspect in the next verse. When God tells them, "Return unto Me and I will return unto you," He is talking about the firstfruits—tithes and offerings.

God is describing the Sin of Adam, which is stealing.

In verse 7, God is describing the Sin of Adam, which is stealing. Adam is to return to God what is His. Instead, Adam steals from God.

Will a Man Rob God?

By eating the fruit, Adam steals the firstfruits offering (the tithe). The proof is in the next verse:

"Will a man rob God? Yet ye have robbed me. But ye say, Wherein have we robbed thee? In tithes and offerings."

Malachi 3:8, KJV

God asks the question, "Will a man rob God?" God is talking about the same sin that Adam commits.

God is asking, "Will you steal from God?"

The same principle set forth here in Malachi is the original sin of Adam—Adam steals from the Tree of the Knowledge of Good and Evil. Adam robs God. He knowingly eats the fruit that is not his, thus failing to make a firstfruits offering to God.

God asks the question, "Will a man rob God?"

Therefore, God says,

> *"I am the LORD, I do not change"* (v. 6).
> *"Return to Me, and I will return to you"* (v. 7).

Man's response is,

> *"But ye said, Wherein shall we return?"* (v. 7 KJV) *and "Wherein have we robbed thee?"* (v. 8 KJV).

This response is the same as someone saying today, "What does that mean? How can You say You will return? How have we robbed You?" The answer to these questions is found at the close of verse 8:

> *"In tithes and offerings."*

Notice God does not say "your" tithes and offerings. You are not giving Him anything that belongs to you when giving tithes and offerings. They already belong to Him. God is saying, "Do not rob Me of tithes and offerings. When you return to Me the tithes and offerings, I will return to you." Return what? FIRSTFRUITS!

Continuing with verses 9-11:

> *"'You are cursed with a curse, for you have robbed Me, even this whole nation. Bring all the tithes into the storehouse, that there may be food in My house, and try Me now in this,' says the LORD of hosts, 'If I will not open for you the windows of heaven and pour out for you such blessing that there will not be room enough to receive it. And I will rebuke the devourer for your sakes, so that he will not destroy the fruit of your ground, nor shall the vine fail to bear fruit for you in the field,' says the LORD of hosts."*

We see here in Malachi, as in Genesis with Adam, that the origin of the problem is stealing from God. God is saying, "If you are not returning unto Me the firstfruits, then you are stealing from Me, and it is the same sin Adam got into. However, if you will prove Me and return the firstfruits, I will return to you. In fact, I will open the windows of heaven and pour the blessing back to you. Because your attitude is proper, I will rebuke the Devil on your behalf, so he cannot steal any of your harvest."

Now, some of you reading this are already tithers, and I am sure you are agreeing wholeheartedly with what I am saying. In contrast, there are some of you who are thinking, "Oh gee, Pastor Billy is just trying to get me to give tithes and offerings." No, no, you have already lied and self-deceived yourself so much because you have been robbing from God, that it is probably hard for me to get through unless the Holy Spirit intervenes. By thinking that, you fall into the same category as those in Malachi who question God, "Wherein shall we return? Wherein have we robbed thee?"

God says, "Return unto Me that which is Mine, and I will return unto you. Prove Me in this and see if I will not open the windows of heaven and pour out the BLESSING." See what He is saying? Since it is presented so simply here, why are so many people self-deceived? It is the way of Cain in manifestation.

THAT WHICH CAUSES US TO REDEFINE WHAT IS ACCEPTABLE TO GOD IS THE WAY OF CAIN

Now, look what happens when people steal from God the firstfruits. Continuing in Malachi:

> *"'Your words have been harsh against Me,' says the LORD, 'Yet you say, "What have we spoken against You?" You have said, "It is useless to serve God; what profit is it that we have kept His ordinance, and that we have walked as mourners before the LORD of hosts?"*
>
> *"'So now we call the proud blessed, for those who do wickedness are raised up; they even tempt God and go free.'"*

Malachi 3:13-15

> *The people who steal from God call the wicked, "blessed"!*

The people who steal from God call the wicked, "blessed"! Notice the spiritual progression. When a person begins stealing firstfruits from God, they attempt to justify their behavior by saying things like, "Why should I tithe? God blesses me anyway." In other words, they are saying, "God blesses me in sin." That is prideful, arrogant, and it is a progression that happens. Soon, these self-deceived people, who do not return the firstfruits unto God, will find that they make excuses as to why. They look at the ungodly and call them "blessed" and say, "See, they do not give their first-fruits and God blesses them." Then they say, "God blesses me anyway."

When someone begins talking about God blessing them in sin, they accuse God of blessing sin. That person is self-deceived. Look at Malachi 3:15 from the *New Living Translation*:

> "*From now on we will call the arrogant blessed. For those who do evil get rich, and those who dare God to punish them suffer no harm.*"

A person will use their mouth out of the midst of their own self-deception, thinking they can redefine what is acceptable to God.

In other words, a person will use their mouth out of the midst of their own self-deception, thinking they can redefine what is acceptable to God. Instead of simply doing what God says, "Return unto Me, and I will return unto you," they will come up with something on their own in an attempt to get a blessing.

We must ask ourselves, "Why do people NOT follow God's instructions when they are so simple?" My answer is the same:

THAT WHICH CAUSES US TO REDEFINE WHAT IS ACCEPTABLE TO GOD IS THE WAY OF CAIN

CHAPTER 4

The Sin of Cain

The Sin of Cain is the same as the Sin of Adam, which is stealing. However, the Sin of Cain is a progression of Adam's sin. The Sin of Adam was most likely a one-time occurrence, while the Sin of Cain set the course for spiritual rebellion.

The Sin of Cain set the course for spiritual rebellion.

To examine the Sin of Cain, let us begin reading from the book of Genesis.

*"Now Adam knew Eve his wife, and she conceived and bore Cain, and said, 'I have acquired a man from the LORD.' Then she bore again, this time his brother Abel. Now **Abel was***

*a keeper of sheep, but **Cain**
was a tiller of the ground."*

Genesis 4:1-2

Abel was a keeper of sheep, but Cain was a tiller of the ground.

I am not sure about you, but I always read into this passage of Scripture that Abel somehow has a better "call" than Cain. The Scripture does not say that. It just tells us their occupations. Abel is a keeper of sheep. Cain is a tiller of the ground.

So, we need not assume that Abel has a good occupation that allows him to give a good offering, but Cain does not. Continuing with verse 3:

*"And **in the process of time** it came to pass that Cain brought an offering of the fruit of the ground to the LORD."*

Notice verse 3 says, "in the process of time." Other translations say it like this, *"when it was time for the harvest"* (NLT).

At harvest time, Cain brings an offering unto the Lord. Notice the Scripture just says "an offering." That is significant. Abel's offering is described in verses 4-5:

"Abel also brought of the firstborn of his flock and of their fat. And the LORD respected Abel and his offering, but He did not respect Cain and his offering."

Abel brings the firstborn of his flock as an offering to the Lord. A "firstborn" is a first-fruits offering.

When harvest time comes, Cain does not bring the firstfruits. He just brings "an offering" of fruit. In fact, in Texas we have a term called "nubs." Cain brings God the nubs. In other words, he brings

Cain brings God the nubs.

God some *leftovers*. Cain does not bring the firstfruits or Scripture would say that he did.

It has been taught that the reason Abel's sacrifice is acceptable is because it is *blood* and Cain's is not; however, the offering of a blood sacrifice is under the Levitical priesthood and is not yet in existence during this account. So, it is not the blood that makes Abel's offering acceptable; it is because Abel offers up the firstborn (firstfruits).

Cain just makes "an offering." No mention of first-fruits. If he does not bring the firstfruits, then we can conclude that he has already eaten some of the food and, consequently, stole the firstfruits offering. As such, when he presents it to God, God has no respect for it. It is disrespectful not to offer the firstfruits. Therefore, the Sin of Cain is not presenting and returning to God the firstfruits. He is committing the same sin of his father, Adam. Continuing with verse 5:

> *"He* [God] *did not respect Cain and his offering. And Cain was very angry, and his countenance fell."*

We see here that when God does not accept Cain's offering, Cain becomes very angry and downcast.

Continuing with verse 6-9:

> *"So the LORD said to Cain, 'Why are you angry? And why has your countenance fallen? If you do well, will you not be accepted? And if you do not do well, sin lies at the door. And its desire is for you, but you should rule over it.'*
>
> *"Now Cain talked with Abel his brother; and it came to pass, when they were in the field, that Cain rose up against Abel his brother and killed him.*
>
> *"Then the LORD said to Cain, 'Where is Abel your brother?' He said, 'I do not know. Am I my brother's keeper?'"*

I believe it is safe to assume that God knows where Abel is and what happened before asking Cain this question. God says to Cain, "Where is Abel your brother?" Cain answers, "I do not know. Am I my brother's keeper?"

Notice Cain and Abel both bring an offering to the Lord. Both of them have instructions on making offerings—most likely from their father, Adam. Adam must have certainly learned his lesson about the importance of firstfruits offerings. It would be unfair for Abel to have knowledge that Cain did not or for God to hold Cain to the same standard as Abel if he did not know. God is no respecter of persons (Acts 10:34). Therefore, we can conclude that God's lack of respect for Cain's offering derives from Cain not following instructions.

Cain knew what he was supposed to offer to God.

Cain knows what he is supposed to offer to God. He knows what is acceptable, but Cain *chooses* to offer something besides the firstfruits. Therefore, he disrespects the commandment and the Word that God gave him through Adam. As a result, God has no respect for his offering.

The only acceptable offering is a firstfruits offering.

THE WAY OF CAIN

Now pay attention, this is what I want you to catch.

Why does Cain disrespect God and make an unacceptable offering?

Cain knows what to offer. So why does he bring an offering to God that IS NOT what God tells him to bring? Then why is he ANGRY when God says, "That offering is not going to work. It is unacceptable!"?

Why does Cain disrespect God and make an unacceptable offering?

This is the answer: **Cain brings his offering FULLY EXPECTING God to accept it.** Otherwise, he would not have become angry when God did not accept his offering. It is here that Cain's spiritual condition is revealed.

Cain is self-deceived into thinking that God will accept his offering EVEN THOUGH it is not a firstfruits offering. His attitude of heart is to redefine what is acceptable to God and expect God to bless him.

THAT WHICH CAUSES US TO REDEFINE WHAT IS ACCEPTABLE TO GOD IS THE WAY OF CAIN

Again, we see the progression of steal—kill—destroy. Cain steals the firstfruits, which kills his relationship with God, and destroys the blessings that follow.

I do not believe Cain considers the possibility that God will not accept his offering. He would have to be extremely arrogant and proud to offer something to God that he knows will not be accepted. No, Cain does not do that. The Sin of Cain is stealing, not arrogance. He steals from God and then offers up leftovers. I do

The Sin of Cain is stealing, not arrogance.

not believe he thinks he is doing wrong. He must think, "God will like this—I am making an effort—it is good food," but God says, "I am the Lord, and I change not. Return to Me the firstfruits (tithes and offerings), and I will return to you (blessings)." Anything else is stealing and starts a spiritual progression of steal, kill, and destroy.

Cain deceives himself into thinking God will accept his offering, even though he does not follow God's instructions. He is self-deceived.

BELIEVING YOU CAN
STEAL FROM GOD
AND THEN REDEFINE WHAT IS
ACCEPTABLE TO GOD
IS THE WAY OF CAIN

In the next chapter, you will find out what Jude, the brother of Jesus, has to say about this spiritual condition.

CHAPTER 5

The Spots in Your Love Feasts

The book of Jude is a little book with only one chapter. It is right next to the final book of the Bible, the book of Revelation. Most theologians agree that Jude was the brother of Jesus. The Word tells us that James and Jesus were brothers as were James and Jude. This would make Jude the brother of Jesus, as well.

Through the Scriptures, we learn that the brothers of Jesus do not believe Him to be the Messiah during His ministry (John 7:3-5). It is not until later that they believe He is the Son of God. However, once they believe, they are convinced!

Since Jude is one of Jesus' brothers, Jude has first-hand knowledge about Jesus—including His ways and teachings. It is Jude who warns about the "way of Cain" that we first read about in Chapter 2. Let us examine that Scripture further:

*"Woe to them! For they have gone in the **way of Cain** . . ."*

Jude 11

What does Jude mean when he writes, "they have gone in the way of Cain"? Is he referring to the first murder? Is he talking specifically about Cain raising up and slaying Abel, or is he explaining something much larger?

*"Woe to them! For they have gone in the **way of Cain**, have run greedily in the error of Balaam for profit, and perished in the rebellion of Korah. These are **spots** in your love feasts."*

Jude 11-12

As previously mentioned, the "spots" that Jude speaks of are *deceptions*. The apostle Peter provides more information concerning these spots. In the following passage, Peter is talking about Noah and Lot and how God knows how to deliver the godly out of temptation and evil. He warns of the fate of those who walk in the flesh and despise authority. The Word says of them,

*"But these, like natural brute beasts made to be caught and destroyed, speak evil of the things they do not understand, and will utterly perish in their own corruption, and will receive the wages of unrighteousness, as those who count it pleasure to carouse in the daytime. They are **spots and blemishes**, carousing in their own **deceptions** while they feast with you, having eyes full of adultery and that cannot cease from sin, enticing unstable souls."*

2 Peter 2:12-14

The "spots and blemishes" are tied with "deceptions." Then he says, *"while they feast with you."* These spots and blemishes are in the midst of us. This passage of Scripture is saying that, "in the midst of our love feasts, there can be spots and blemishes who are basking in their deceptions. The spots and blemishes are deceived people.

The spots and blemishes are deceived people.

Let us look again at our passage in Jude. Jude says,

"Woe to them! For they have gone in the way of Cain, have run greedily in the error of Balaam for profit, and perished in the rebellion

of Korah. These are spots in your love feasts, **while they feast with you** *without fear, serving only themselves."*

Jude 11-12

Notice the two different people feasting together: one *without* spot and blemish, and another that *is* a spot and blemish. The opening phrase, "Woe to them!" means "alas" or "what sorrow or sadness." In other words, it says, "Alas, look at what is taking place!" Then it gives us three directions in which the "spots and blemishes" have gone astray: (1) the way of Cain; (2) the greed of Balaam, and (3) the rebellion of Korah.

The Greed of Balaam

The "greed of Balaam" has become very obvious in our day and hour. We can see the result of the greed of Balaam all around us. We have corporate greed wherein many companies have mistreated their staff causing unions to form. While the unions were formed with good purpose and intent, many unions have also become greedy and corrupt. Then the government stepped in to help; likewise, the government got into greed and corruption.

There is also personal greed, greed in our financial institutions, the auto industry, everything! Greed runs rampant. So, the greed of Balaam is obvious to us all.

Second Peter 2:14-15 describes these people as "accursed children" who, for dishonest rewards and gain, love unrighteousness more than God's righteousness. Their love of money and power causes them to ignore, or distort, the Word of God for financial gain.

The Rebellion of Korah

The rebellion of Korah refers to an account in the book of Numbers wherein a man named Korah rebels—and incites others to rebel—against the authority of Moses and Aaron.

"They gathered together [Korah and company] *against Moses and Aaron, and said to them, 'You take too much upon yourselves, for all the congregation is holy, every one of them, and the LORD is among them. Why then do you exalt yourselves above the assembly of the LORD?'"*

Numbers 16:3

Korah is saying, "We will do whatever we want to do. Who says we have to listen you?!" By rebelling against the leadership and authority God had established during the time of Moses, these men sealed their own fate:

> *"And the earth opened its mouth and swallowed them up, with their households and all the men with Korah, with all their goods. So they and all those with them went down alive into the pit; the earth closed over them, and they perished from among the assembly."*
>
> Numbers 16:32-33

We have never seen a time on the face of this earth that rebellion has run as rampantly as today.

By reading this account, we can easily determine that God considers rebellion a serious offense. Yet, we have never seen a time on the face of this earth that rebellion has run as rampantly as today. We constantly witness people rebelling against authority, law enforcement, and leadership on the news, on television programs, and in our communities. It is as if people really believe it is understandable to rebel. We see it in children, adults, and churches. Thank God, not in my church! I pray it is not in your church either.

The Way of Cain

We see the greed of Balaam and the rebellion of Korah currently being played out on the world stage, but what about the "way of Cain"? The "way of Cain" referred to by Jude, is not just referring to the murder Cain commits, or the fact that God has no respect for his offering. Those aspects are included, but what I want you to see is the *spirit* that drives Cain. It is the reason he redefines what he thinks is acceptable to God. He presents an offering to God that is not the firstfruits, but leftovers, and expects God to accept it. It is the spiritual attitude that allows Cain to become self-deceived. This is the *way of Cain.*

As we have discovered, the way of Cain is a spiritual condition that causes people to become self-deceived to the point of redefining what is acceptable to God. Whatever God tells us in His Word is the final word. It is not up to us to redefine what He says or what we believe to be acceptable.

CHAPTER 6

Jesus Warns of Deceptions

Let us once again look at Peter's description of "spots and blemishes":

"And [they] *will receive the wages of unrighteousness, as those who count it pleasure to carouse in the daytime. They are* **spots and blemishes***, carousing in their own* **deceptions** *while they feast with you."*

2 Peter 2:13

Jesus prophesies about His return, the end of times, and the destruction of the temple:

"Then Jesus went out and departed from the temple, and His disciples came up to show Him

the buildings of the temple. And Jesus said to them, 'Do you not see all these things? Assuredly, I say to you, not one stone shall be left here upon another, that shall not be thrown down.'"

Matthew 24:1-2

In response, the disciples come to Him and say,

"Tell us, when will these things be? And what will be the sign of Your coming, and of the end of the age?"

Matthew 24:3

They are asking Jesus when these things will happen and when will He return. Jesus answers them and says,

*"Take heed that no one **deceives** you. For many will come in My name, saying, 'I am the Christ,' and will **deceive** many. And you will hear of wars and rumors of wars. See that you are not troubled; for all these things must come to pass, but the end is not yet. For nation will rise against nation, and kingdom against kingdom. And there will be famines, pesti- lences, and earthquakes in various places . . . then many false prophets will rise up and **deceive** many . . . For false christs and false*

*prophets will rise and show great signs and wonders to **deceive**, if possible, even the elect."*

Matthew 24:4-7, 11, 24

Notice Jesus mentions criteria such as wars, rumors of wars, nation against nation, pestilences, and earthquakes only once. Yet, He mentions "deception" four times. Jesus is saying, "Let no man deceive you," "Many are going to come, but do not be deceived," and "Many will be deceived." So, we see that our biggest enemy is not another nation, wars, rumors of wars, pestilences, or earthquakes. Our biggest enemy is DECEPTION.

Self-Deception

Please listen to me carefully. **The highest form of deception is self-deception.** Now we know that the Devil is the deceiver, and we know to deceive is to mislead, but the highest form of deception is self-deception. That is, when you deceive yourself.

The highest form of deception is self-deception.

In order to break free from self-deception, you must first identify that *you are* deceived, and then take heed to the Word of God and repent. Afterwards, there is generally a process of recovery that must take place. However, it would not be accurate to state simply, "The way of Cain is self-deception," because it is self-deception in a specific direction, which we will examine in the next Chapter.

"If anyone among you thinks he is religious, and does not bridle his tongue but deceives his own heart, this one's religion is useless."

James 1:26

In this verse, James speaks of someone who does not watch their words. One of the ways one becomes self-deceived is by not watching what comes out of their mouth. By not lining your mouth up with the Word of God, your religion is useless even though you may think you are religious.

When you hear the Word and do not do it, you actually deceive yourself.

"But be doers of the word, and not hearers only, deceiving yourselves."

James 1:22

When you hear the Word and do not do it, you actually deceive yourself. Not doing what the Word tells you to do is a form of self-deception. Let us look at another Scripture:

"For if anyone thinks himself to be something, when he is nothing, he deceives himself."

Galatians 6:3

What Paul is speaking of here is simple: PRIDE! If you think of yourself more highly than you should be, then you are in pride and self-deception.

So, we have looked at three ways of becoming self-deceived: (1) not watching the words coming out of your mouth; (2) hearing the Word, but not doing the Word; and (3) thinking of yourself more highly than you should be, which is pride.

CHAPTER 7

Breaking the Cycle of Self-Deception

As we have discovered, the definition of the way of Cain is being self-deceived into thinking you can redefine what is acceptable to God. Based on the law of spiritual progression, the root of the way of Cain is stealing from God.

The same spiritual disposition that caused the downfall of Cain has been exposed by the Spirit of the Lord in the Body of Christ.

The Body of Christ is full of church people who think they can redefine what is acceptable to

The Body of Christ is full of church people who think they can redefine what is acceptable to God.

God, even though God has already told us through His Word what He expects. It has already been laid out for us. It is forever settled in heaven and earth.

"For assuredly, I say to you, till heaven and earth pass away, one jot or one tittle will by no means pass from the law till all is fulfilled."

Matthew 5:18

This Scripture means the Word of God has been set and established FOREVER. No ifs, ands, or buts. You do not ever have to wonder what God thinks about any subject He addresses in His Word. However, throughout the Body of Christ, we see people trying to redefine what God says in His Word, and then self-deceive themselves into believing it is okay with God. IT IS NOT!

As someone who loves you, I am going to go ahead and tell you straight: **If this is you and you do not get this manifestation of the way of Cain stopped in your life right now, it will follow you for as long as you will allow it to deceive you.**

Blessings will pass you by—life will pass you by—the good will pass you by, and you will still be redefining what is acceptable to God because you are self-deceived.

Remember the man we discussed earlier in this book? The one who does not see good when it comes?

"Cursed is the man who trusts in man and makes flesh his strength, whose heart departs from the LORD. For he shall be like a shrub in the desert, and shall not see when good comes."

Jeremiah 17:5-6

THAT WHICH BLINDS YOU TO NOT SEE GOOD WHEN IT COMES IS THE WAY OF CAIN

This man redefines what is acceptable to God. His heart departs from the Lord, and he puts his trust in man and the flesh. He does not see goodness and blessings when they come by. The way of Cain blinds him to the blessings of God.

If God tells us to do something in the Word, then what right do you or I have to rethink or redefine it? We have discussed the sin of Korah's rebellion and the greed of Balaam, but how about pride? How about the arrogance of trying to rethink and redefine God's plan?

Are You Redefining God's Word?

One area throughout the Body of Christ where we see this kind of pride is in the area of tithing. The Word says a tithe is one-tenth. Therefore, one-tenth is what we all should tithe. No one has the right to redefine what is acceptable to God and then ask Him to bless it. **He has told you what to do, but you may want to offer something else to Him—just like Cain!**

Now, if you have *never* tithed or been a giver, and you do not know how to do it, then the way of Cain has blinded you. Repent! Get it out of your life and start giving and doing what you can. Do something, because you have self-deceived yourself into thinking it is okay to do nothing. "God still loves me!" Yes, He loves you, but goodness is passing you by—life is passing you by—current blessings are passing you by. All the while, death, cursing, and everything else that seems to be overshadowing you is happening because you are self-deceived. It is the way of Cain!

I am writing prophetically to the Body of Christ right now. **For many of you, the blessing, the glory, and the anointing that is supposed to be in your life is passing you by because you are self-deceived.**

Choosing Not to Attend Church

If you are one who does not want to go to church, I just have one question for you: Who told you that you could redefine whether or not you go to church?

"And let us consider one another in order to stir up love and good works, not forsaking the assembling of ourselves together, as is the manner of some, but exhorting one another, and so much the more as you see the Day approaching."

Hebrews 10:24-25

Who told you that you could redefine whether or not you go to church?

The Word has already told us to gather together. Who are you to redefine whether or not going to church is acceptable to God? God has told you through his Word not to forsake assembling together in the church. Yes, you need to study, pray, and go about doing good, but He also told you not to forsake assembling together.

Do Not Be Deceived

You are self-deceived if you think that you can redefine whether or not we assemble together. You are self-deceived if you think you can redefine what is acceptable in your giving. God has already told you in the Word. Who are you to redefine it? Just obey!

We do not trust in man and in what we see.

Do not forsake tithing, giving to the poor, or giving for the Gospel's sake. You are to give your best unto God. When hard times hit, many people stop giving to churches and ministries when it should be a time when giving increases. When we experience drought, it is a time to plant more seed. We trust this principle because we are not self-deceived. We do not trust in man and in what we see. We trust in what God says in the Word:

> *"Give, and it will be given to you: good measure, pressed down, shaken together, and running over will be put into your bosom. For with the same measure that you use, it will be measured back to you."*
>
> Luke 6:38

If you think it is okay to decrease your giving when times get tough, you are self-deceived. That is the way of Cain operating in your life.

God declares in His Word what is acceptable. Look in your Bible and find out for yourself what that is. If you do not agree and do not act upon it, anything else you decree is unacceptable. If you decree what His Word says, then you and God are in agreement and therein lies the power:

"So shall my word be that goeth forth out of my mouth: it shall not return unto me void, but it shall accomplish that which I please, and it shall prosper in the thing whereto I sent it."

Isaiah 55:11, KJV

God's Word declares what is acceptable, what is expected, and what it takes to be like a tree planted by the rivers of water (remember the blessed man of Jeremiah 17:7-8). We do not have the privilege of redefining His expectations.

Do Not Be Like Cain

Let me tell you what the way of Cain says, "Well, God loves me and accepts me the way I am. I don't have to change. In fact, I don't have to give, I don't have to tithe, and I don't have to give for the Gospel's sake to ministries. I don't have to give to the poor. After all, am I my brother's keeper?"

For you to redefine what is acceptable to God, is saying, "I don't have to keep up with my brother." Cain was so self-deceived that he thought he could offer whatever he wanted. He thought he could redefine what God says, and God would say, "Oh, thank you Cain, wow, some leftover fruit!"

Break the Way of Cain

The Body of Christ has to break any manifestation of the way of Cain. You have to stop stealing from God the firstfruits. If you downplay this message in your mind because you think I just want your tithes and offerings, remember, they are not mine—they belong to God.

Brother Kenneth Copeland taught me that if a man does not handle his finances correctly, neither will he handle the anointing correctly.

The presentation of fruitfruits unto God puts you in right relationship with Him.

"Therefore if you have not been faithful in the unrighteous mammon, who will commit to your trust the true riches?"

Luke 16:11

This message is not intended for the purpose of gaining tithes and offerings; it is intended for you to gain the necessary knowledge to present unto God that which is God's. After that, He can open the windows of heaven on your behalf. The presentation of fruitfruits unto God puts you in right relationship with Him.

I will admit the assignment of God on my life, and that of every other pastor, would be much easier if the Body of Christ were in right relationship with the Lord. If such were the case, we could reach into spiritual things that have been, up to now, unobtainable because we cannot BREAK THROUGH THE SIN!

No, this is not a message on tithes and offerings; it is a message on firstfruits and obedience.

God says, "I am the Lord, and I change not. Return to Me the firstfruits (tithes and offerings), and I will return to you." Anything else is stealing and starts a spiritual progression of steal—kill—destroy.

Remember, when you steal the firstfruits:

- You kill your relationship, right standing, and connection with God;

- You begin speaking wrong things about God, usually expecting Him to bless you in your sin (robbery); and

- You destroy the blessing that God wants to return and pour out on your life.

It is God's wish for you to have an abundant life. I do not want to see your relationship or your harvest hindered by that deceiving way of Cain anymore.

When Cain got angry, upset, and his countenance fell, then God gave him a chance to repent. God said, "Why are you angry?" That was an invitation. "Talk to Me, Cain. Come to Me." Cain could have repented right then, saying, "Forgive me. I have stolen the firstfruits. I ask You to forgive me Lord." At that moment, God would have accepted his repentance. It would have been a completely different writing about Cain.

What will God's history books have to say about you? You can decide your future right now. You can CHOOSE LIFE!

Conclusion

If you want to be fruitful, then you are going to have to break any manifestation of the way of Cain operating in your life. The hold may be stronger on some than others, or it may not be in you at all. Maybe, it has consumed you.

I am calling heaven and earth to record today. I have set before you the Word. I have explained to you, as a watchman on the wall, the manifestations of the way of Cain:

THAT WHICH CAUSES ONE TO:

NOT SEE GOOD WHEN IT COMES

STEAL FROM GOD

REDEFINE WHAT IS ACCEPTABLE TO GOD

IS THE WAY OF CAIN

So, by the authority of the name of Jesus Christ of Nazareth, I break that way of Cain over you. I command it to be broken! I release freedom and healing. I call you to repentance, and I ask for your eyes to be enlightened and all darkness removed. I break that spirit of darkness and rulers of darkness over you, NOW! In the name of Jesus Christ of Nazareth, receive your blessing! Receive your freedom!

Do not allow the way of Cain to enter your life, family, business, or church. We know by the Word that you must first bind the strongman before you can spoil his house.

"No one can enter a strong man's house and plunder his goods, unless he first binds the strong man. And then he will plunder his house."

Mark 3:27

Now that you know the truth, having true repentance of self-deception is up to you. Do not be angry like Cain. This is your chance to repent.

If you believe the way of Cain has been affecting your life and you have repented, you should NOT have that spirit anymore. You will have to resist it if it comes near you again, but now you will be able to recognize it by its manifestations and STOMP IT OUT! Do not let the blessings and goodness of God pass you by—the price is too expensive to pay.

Prayer of Repentance

If this is you and you would like to pray this prayer with me, please do so:

Father, in the name of Jesus Christ of Nazareth, I bind that way of Cain that has been coming against me. I renounce that sin and release it from me right now. I repent for trying to redefine what is acceptable to You.

Right now, I not only receive Your forgiveness, I declare and decree that I am free from that spirit. I will never again compromise Your Word for any reason.

The way of Cain is not welcome in my life, my home, my church, or my place of business. I am not deceived, but have my eyes open to Your goodness and the blessing that You send my way.

Thank you, Heavenly Father. In Jesus' name, Amen.

ABOUT THE AUTHOR

Dr. Billy J. Rash is Senior Pastor of Kern Christian Center in Bakersfield, California. He earned a Doctorate of Divinity from Southern California Theological Seminary and a Doctorate of Theology from Vision Christian University.

After accepting the Lord and receiving the baptism of the Holy Spirit in the early 1970s, Pastor Billy Rash was introduced to the faith message through the ministry of Kenneth Copeland. Pastor Billy went to work for Kenneth Copeland Ministries as an Associate Minister in 1978. If Gloria Copeland could not attend a meeting, then Pastor Billy would teach the healing school and participate in the miracle services with Brother Copeland.

In the following years, he began evangelizing under Billy Rash Ministries. In 1985, Pastor Billy moved to Bakersfield and started a new church, Kern Christian Center.

In addition to his duties as Senior Pastor, he is also involved in community service as Chaplain for the Bakersfield Police Department. He is also an advisory-board member for Hilton Sutton World Ministries and on the President's Cabinet for Jerry Savelle Ministries. Pastor Billy is married to Shelby Rash, and they make their home in Bakersfield, California.

Audio and video messages from Pastor Billy
can be accessed via the Internet at
www.kernchristiancenter.org.

For more information, please contact:

Billy Rash Ministries
7850 White Lane, No. 117
Bakersfield, California 93309
(661) 664-1000

www.billyrashministries.org